MW00988619

TONY EVANS

Speaks Out On

BEING SINGLE & SATISFIED

TONY EVANS

Speaks Out On

BEING SINGLE & SATISFIED

MOODY PUBLISHERS

CHICAGO

© 2002 by
ANTHONY T. EVANS

All rights reserved. No part of this book may be reproduced in any form without permission in writing from the publisher, except in the case of brief quotations embodied in critical articles or reviews.

All Scripture quotations are taken from the *New American Standard Bible*®, © Copyright The Lockman Foundation 1960, 1962, 1963, 1968, 1971, 1972, 1973, 1975, 1977, 1995. Used by permission.

ISBN: 978-0-8024-4371-7

We hope you enjoy this book from Moody Publishers. Our goal is to provide high-quality, thought-provoking books and products that connect truth to your real needs and challenges. For more information on other books and products written and produced from a biblical perspective, go to www.moodypublishers.com or write to:

Moody Publishers
820 N. LaSalle Boulevard
Chicago, IL 60610

7 9 10 8 6

Printed in the United States of America

BEING SINGLE AND SATISFIED

A single woman was talking with her pastor one day, discussing the subject of marriage. The pastor said, "You know, God has designed the perfect plan for marriage, one man and one woman together for life. You can't improve on God's plan."

"Pastor, I don't want to improve on it," the woman replied. "I just want to get in on it."

That's the way many single people feel today. They fear they are missing out on God's plan or God's best for their lives because they aren't married. Many singles feel as if their lives are in a holding pattern, like an airplane that is supposed to be landing at its destination but has been ordered to circle the airport.

I've flown enough to know what it's like for the pilot to come on the intercom and announce that the plane has been denied permission to land for whatever reason. Holding patterns are very frustrating because you are helpless. You didn't choose the situation, and there is nothing you can do about it. All you know is that you want the pilot to get that metal bird on the ground so you can get off and get on with your life.

If you are a Christian single person who loves God and wants to honor and serve Him with your life, then I want to speak to you from God's Word, because the Bible contains some very important, challenging, and encouraging principles for Christian singles. (Let me also say that these principles have implications for married people, as we'll see.)

The Scripture deals with the subject of singleness head-on in 1 Corinthians 7:25–40, where the apostle Paul was in the process of answering his readers' questions concerning marriage and singleness. Paul was the right person to handle these issues, because the evidence suggests that he had been married at one time and then lived for many years as a single person. So he knew what it was like to have a mate and to be alone.

Paul must have been married because before his conversion he was a member of the Sanhedrin, the supreme council of Jewish leaders, which required its members to be married. Perhaps his wife had died, or she may even have left him when he came to Christ. The point is that Paul knew what it was like both to have a mate and to live as a single person.

There's another reason 1 Corinthians 7 is so important to the issue of marital status, which is that Paul was speaking by divine revelation. So what he wrote in this portion of Scripture is the Word of God and not just one man's opinion. And in 1 Corinthians 7 we find at least three vital principles for singles. We can summarize these as waiting on the Lord, working for the Lord, and being wed in the Lord.

WAITING ON THE LORD

A lot of singles would look at this subhead and say, "Oh, yeah, I know all about waiting. I've been waiting on the Lord to give me a mate for a long time."

Most singles would agree that they're waiting for an opportunity to marry, because they don't plan on being single the rest of their lives. God's concern for you as a waiting single is *how you are doing* while you're waiting. Let me show you what I mean.

Paul had been discussing marriage and divorce in 1 Corinthians 7:1–24 before turning to the specific issue of singleness in verse 25: "Now concerning virgins I have no command of the Lord, but I give an opinion as one who by the mercy of the Lord is trustworthy."

When Paul said the Lord had not given a command about being single, he meant that when Jesus was on earth He didn't speak directly to this issue. Jesus certainly could have spoken on singleness, because He experienced the single life to the nth degree, including the temptations that singles face.

But God chose instead to entrust His message on singleness and its principles to Paul. My point is that when Paul said he was offering his view, he was saying, "I have the Lord's mind on this." This is important because some people try to discount Paul's teaching here as of lesser authority than Jesus' words. But the Bible knows no such distinction.

Wait in Moral Purity

Notice that when Paul began to discuss unmarried people, he used the term *virgins* in 1 Corinthians 7:25. For Paul, singleness was synonymous with virginity, and so the first principle in waiting is to maintain your moral purity.

In the divine context, if you are single and you love the Lord, you are also celibate. The two go hand in hand. Paul was referring primarily to physical virginity or sexual purity, although there is also a spiritual purity that people who have been sexually immoral can re-capture. We'll talk about that too.

God not only anticipates and expects, but also de-mands, that single people be celibate. Now this is a dif-ficult message in a day of license, liberty, and hedonism. We've gone from the Victorian Age to Victoria's Secret catalogs and television ads. Modesty has been thrown to the wind. Yet we are not called to adapt the Bible to our age, but to adapt our age to the Bible.

Sex today has been cheapened by a world that does not have a divine perspective. And things that are cheap can be given away easily. Things that are valu-able, you protect.

My single friend, your sense of value will be meas-ured in large part by your morality. Too many people treat sex like the all-night drive-through at the local fast-food restaurant—always available when the desire hits you. Purity is no longer a priority.

But the Bible says equally to men and to women that God's desire and design for singles is their moral purity. Sex in God's hand is holy; sex in the devil's hand is death. One of the major ways that Satan promotes his program in history is through illicit sex. For example, Satan used sexual relations between unholy men and the "daughters of men" to produce an ungodly race in an attempt to destroy God's plan for the world (see Genesis 6:1–2).

How spiritual is this matter of sex for a Christian?

Since God commands purity for singles, how can a single person come to grips with this demand when our natural desires and our sexuality are so much a part of our makeup? To answer that, let me show you a crucial principle in Paul's thinking that comes out of this same letter to the Corinthians. The principle is that as Christians we are not to view sex as purely a biological matter, but as a spiritual one.

In 1 Corinthians 6:13 Paul wrote, "Food is for the stomach and the stomach is for food, but God will do away with both of them. Yet the body is not for immorality, but for the Lord, and the Lord is for the body."

Notice the contrast between the way we treat hunger, a legitimate physical appetite, and the way we should treat our bodies when it comes to sexual morality. Most people in Corinth, a very wicked city, equated food with sex. When they got hungry, they ate. When they wanted sex, they fed that appetite. Corinth even had a temple with a restaurant on one side and a brothel on the other. A person could have dinner at the restaurant and go to the brothel for dessert. No big deal.

No, Paul says, it's a very big deal. It's OK to eat when you're hungry because the stomach was made for food. But it's not OK to indulge in sex whenever you feel like it because your body was not made for sexual immorality. This is where Paul begins to make the switch from the purely physical to the spiritual view of sex—which he will expand on in verses 15–20.

But notice verse 14, which explains how singles can remain sexually pure when everything around them says to go ahead and indulge their appetites. "Now God has not only raised the Lord, but will also raise us up through His power."

This might seem out of place at first. What does Christ's resurrection and our future resurrection have to do with a Christian's sexual purity? Everything, because Paul is saying that we have the same power working within us that raised Jesus from the dead. If God can raise Jesus from the dead, He can give us the power to remain pure even in a decadent culture.

How spiritual is this matter of sex for a Christian? Paul answers that by beginning with a question: "Do you not know that your bodies are members of Christ? Shall I then take away the members of Christ and make them members of a prostitute? May it never be!" (1 Corinthians 6:15).

Why was Paul so adamant about this? Because the truth of our spiritual union with Christ means that whatever we do, we bring Jesus into it with us. In other words, whenever you as a Christian are sexually intimate with another person, you are making Jesus participate with you.

God has given His blessing to sex within the marriage union, but if the sexual activity is outside of marriage it's the equivalent of spiritual rape. Paul was horrified at the thought, and we should be too.

Why is sex so devastating both physically and spiritually when it is misused? We find the answer to that in 1 Corinthians 6:16–18. "Or do you not know that the one who joins himself to a prostitute is one body with her? For He says, 'The two shall become one flesh'" (v. 16). Paul says that a unique spiritual union is created by the sex act, even when it is done as an act of immorality between two people who have no intention of forming a lasting relationship.

We know this because Paul used God's own words from the first marriage (see Genesis 2:24) to describe a temporary sexual union. Even if a man would probably never consider walking down the aisle with a woman he used for a "one-night stand," there is a sense in which he *did* walk down the aisle with her.

To be sure, their union was a false one, but the fact is that their sexual union formed a one-flesh relationship that also included a fusion of their souls. It's as if these two people each stamped a part of his or her soul on the other person. Therefore, when they separate, each leaves behind a part of him or herself with the other person, creating tremendous spiritual damage.

That's why the idea of illicit or casual sex as a one-time encounter that's over and done the next morning is the furthest thing from the truth. Many people who have been sexually immoral can testify to painful memories that play themselves back because God designed sex as a spiritual and not merely a biological reality.

Instead of two people joining themselves together sexually outside of marriage, God has a higher standard: "But the one who joins himself to the Lord is one spirit with Him" (1 Corinthians 6:17). There must be a spiritual oneness with the Lord that overrides the desire for illegitimate physical oneness with another person.

And so God's advice to singles or anyone tempted to engage in illicit activity is "Flee immorality. Every other sin that a man commits is outside the body, but the immoral man sins against his own body" (v. 18). Immorality has a self-destructive effect built into it.

Then Paul asked another important question. "Or do you not know that your body is a temple of the Holy Spirit who is in you, whom you have from God, and that you are not your own? For you have been bought with a price; therefore glorify God in your body" (vv. 19–20).

We can see the spiritual nature of sex here because

Paul referred to our bodies as temples with which we can glorify God. A temple is a church house, the place where God is worshiped. This means that when a husband and wife engage in sex, they are actually participating in an act of worship.

This is an awesome illustration of the spiritual nature of our sexuality. In the Old Testament, a person who wanted to get close to God went into the temple to worship. And in the deepest recess of the temple was a place called the Holy of Holies, the most sacred part of the temple hidden behind a veil. No one could enter there but the high priest, and then only once a year with blood to cover the people's sins.

God has created every woman with a bodily veil called a hymen. This creates a covering that literally says what the Old Testament said about the Holy of Holies—no trespassing until such time as it is appropriate to shed blood.

That's why it is common for a woman who is a virgin to shed blood on her wedding night. There is a breaking of the veil, the hymen, by the only person rightfully allowed to do that, the woman's husband-priest. Sexual intercourse between a husband and wife is a holy act.

What about single men and women who will not be able to know this wedding-night experience in the way God intended because they have already had sex outside of marriage? Let's be clear that illicit sex is sin, but the Bible also has a word of hope and restoration for singles who have failed morally.

Judging from Paul's message in 1 Corinthians, he was writing to a lot of people who had been immoral. No matter what they had done, Paul wrote, "But you were washed, but you were sanctified, but you were justified in the name of the Lord Jesus Christ" (1 Corinthians 6:11).

God can and will forgive sexual sin and restore any believer to purity. Those who have lost their physical virginity can still regain their spiritual virginity and purity of life before God. Spiritual virginity is when God gives you back what the devil took away.

You see, when God saved you He made you a diamond. If I rub a diamond in the dirt, what I have is a dirty diamond that has lost none of its intrinsic value. It just needs to be cleansed and restored to its original luster.

We can't change the past, but we can clean up the present and look forward to a shiny future. If you have compromised your moral purity and have not dealt with it before God, go to Him in confession and repentance and experience His cleansing (read 1 John 1:9 and claim its promise). And if you are still a virgin and committed to sexual purity, ask God to help you stand strong. And remember, He has promised not to let you get in any situation without a way of escape (see 1 Corinthians 10:13).

Wait with the Right Mentality

While you're waiting on the Lord, make sure that your thinking is straight too. Paul addressed this issue in verses 26–28 of 1 Corinthians 7.

Too many singles have only one thought on their minds: *I need to get married, no matter what*. But the Bible has a different emphasis. "I think then that this is good in view of the present distress, that it is good for a man to remain as he is" (v. 26). In other words, whether you're married or single, don't let your marital status dominate your thinking and focus.

Paul said this because he knew there were bigger things at stake in the Christian life than a person's marital status. This wouldn't be such a big deal for singles today except that we are guilty as a society and as a church of making single people feel like second-class citizens.

But God doesn't make any distinction between married and single people in terms of their value in His eyes. That's clear from what Paul said in 1 Corinthians 7:27: "Are you bound to a wife? Do not seek to be released. Are you released from a wife? Do not seek a wife."

If singleness were not as perfectly acceptable to God as marriage, He would have commanded all Christians to get married, and Paul would probably have gotten married, or perhaps remarried, himself. The point is that singles are not worse off than married people.

In fact, marriage has its own set of challenges and problems. "If a virgin marries, she has not sinned. Yet such will have trouble in this life, and I am trying to spare you," Paul wrote in 1 Corinthians 7:28.

Now I know that many single Christians, especially older singles, become defensive when they hear this because they think, *Oh yes, here it comes, the old "You're better off single" speech that's supposed to make me feel better about not having anyone.*

That may be some people's reaction, but there's no denying the truth that from the standpoint of kingdom service, which was Paul's focus, singles are less encumbered than married people.

We also can't deny the truth that marriage is not an automatic fix for all the needs of single people. You may say, "But Tony, I'm lonely. I have to eat alone at night and go to bed alone. I have normal emotional longings and sexual needs that are not being fulfilled, and I'm frustrated."

Well, I've counseled many married people who are so emotionally lonely and/or sexually unsatisfied that they're thinking about bailing out on their marriages and going back to being single. The only thing more painful than being single and miserable is being married and miserable.

Let's get our thinking straight. Anyone who thinks marriage is the be-all and end-all of life, the answer to all of a single person's dreams and problems, is in for a big letdown. Marriage is wonderful, but someone likened it to flies on a window screen. Some are on the outside wanting in, and others are on the inside wanting out.

There's not an honest married person who will not tell you that marriage involves adjustments and problems along with the benefits. The question is not whether marriage or singleness is better but what

God's will is for each of His children in light of eternity's values.

When Paul said, "Do not seek a wife," he wasn't saying it's wrong to desire to be married. Instead, his focus was on methodology. The idea is, "Stop man-hunting or woman-hunting. Don't spend all your time searching for the right one."

Everywhere singles turn today they find someone trying to fix them up with a prospect, whether it's over the Internet, at church, or in the family. Single people used to play "The Dating Game" on television. But some people play it in real life.

You need to connect with the One who knows where the right one is.

You don't have to play that game. Adam found his wife when he was asleep. God put the boy out and crafted a wife for him and then brought Eve to Adam. I say that humorously but also seriously. Single person, God knows where you live. You don't have to spend all your time worrying about tracking down a mate or trying to be in all the right places to meet people. Get on with your life and service for God. He knows where to find you when the time is right.

Again, I'm not saying to avoid social situations or

relationships with other singles. In fact, it's still true that "he who finds a wife finds a good thing" (Proverbs 18:22), which implies that a single man must make an effort to seek a wife if he wants to experience the benefits of marriage. What I'm talking about is the frantic kind of dating in which a single goes from one person to another, hoping one day to bump into the right one but often getting messed up in the search.

I'll never forget a single young woman in our church in Dallas who had it together. She was loving and serving God and minding her own business until one Sunday several years ago when she came to church alone because a friend who usually came with her couldn't make it.

This young woman was sitting in the second row of our family center, where we met for church in those days. A young man came into church that morning and looked for a seat in the back row, which was filled. The ushers escorted him to the front and seated him next to this woman. During the greeting time they said hello to each other—and you can guess the rest. They got married not long after that. It doesn't take long when God sets things up.

That won't happen for everybody, but whether it happens or not, God wants single people to seek Him, not seek a mate in the sense that you're on a mission that comes to dominate your decisions and your commitments. You don't need to find the right one. You need to connect with the One who knows where the right one is.

Singles who are waiting on God with the right kind of thinking know that marriage is not an escape from loneliness or lack of fulfillment or temptation, because there are lonely, unfulfilled, and tempted married people.

If you're thinking this way, God says change your mind. You're all right the way you are. Talk to God about your desires, but don't think there's something wrong with you that will never be fixed unless and until you get married.

Wait with the Right View of Mortality

Waiting on the Lord also involves a proper understanding of your mortality. I'll let the Word explain what I mean:

> But this I say, brethren, the time has been shortened, so that from now on those who have wives should be as though they had none; and those who weep, as though they did not weep, and those who rejoice, as though they did not rejoice, and those who buy, as though they did not possess; and those who use the world, as though they did not make full use of it; for the form of this world is passing away. (1 Corinthians 7:29–31)

Life is too short, the apostle Paul says, to get all hung up on stuff—and even relationships—that are going to pass away when God torches this present world and its system. Remember, God wants us to take the long, that is, the eternal, view of life. Anything that we can't send on ahead into heaven is strictly temporary and destined to pass away.

Paul illustrated his point with several earthly activities, but it's interesting that his first illustration is marriage. This is not a put-down on marriage, but a sober assessment of what counts most in life. Jesus said there will be no marriage in heaven because we will be like the angels, in the sense of being unmarried as they are (see Matthew 22:30).

In other words, marriage will pass away just like other earthly activities such as buying and selling. There is certainly nothing wrong with desiring to be married. Just don't treat marriage as if you'll die unhappy if you don't experience it. We as Christians can't afford to give anything on earth more time or weight than it deserves, or else it will start detracting from our eternal perspective.

I was talking to a single man one day who told me, "I don't want Jesus to rapture me yet. He just needs to delay His coming a little longer because I'm not married yet."

Now he may have been kidding a little bit, but that's a pretty common view among singles. We've already established that there is nothing wrong with singles desiring a mate and developing relationships that could lead to marriage. But when any earthly goal overtakes a heavenly goal, we're vulnerable to making a mistake.

One mistake some Christian singles make when they elevate marriage to the top of their priority list is that they marry an unbeliever. We're going to talk later about what it means to be married "in the Lord" (1 Corinthians 7:39), so let me just mention this one for now because it's a big problem.

Bad things can happen when single people start fixating on marriage to the exclusion of other aspects of life. They begin to think that they're missing out on something good—or, worse, that God is holding out on them because He doesn't love them as much as the Bible says He does.

Singles in that situation are very vulnerable to the same deception that Satan worked on Eve in the Garden of Eden. It was a masterful plan.

Let's say for the sake of illustration that there were one hundred trees in the garden. That meant Eve had ninety-nine beautiful trees to eat from freely, because God only put one tree off-limits, the tree of the knowledge of good and evil.

But you can read about Satan's strategy in Genesis 3. He got Eve to focus and fixate on that one forbidden tree. "G-i-r-r-l-l, you see that tree? Why would God keep that one tree from you if He loves you? He's holding out on you, because He knows that tree will make you be like Him."

What Satan tries to do with singles is put marriage or sex before them and tell them, "If God really cared about you, He wouldn't deprive you of these pleasures. After all, He created them for you. Go ahead and enjoy the fruit."

Too many singles are so hung up on getting married that they never get around to enjoying the whole garden of opportunities and service that God has for them.

That's the difference between a successful single and a defeated single.

Life is too short to focus all of your energies on something that may last thirty or forty years as opposed to the things of God that will last forever.

Now don't misunderstand. It's fine to pray for a mate, desire a mate, and anticipate the day when you will have a mate. If you want to be married, assume that God is going to allow you to be married at some point unless He changes your desire.

But don't forget that He is also preparing you for greater things than just being married. Paul said he had the right to marry a believing woman (see 1 Corinthians 9:5), and no doubt he had thought about it. We tend to canonize and sterilize Paul and forget that he was a man with normal human desires. But Paul surrendered his right to marry for the greater calling of the kingdom of God. God doesn't call everyone to do that, but He does call us to "set [our] mind on the things above, not on the things that are on earth" (Colossians 3:2).

You can do this while you're waiting on the Lord for a husband or wife. You can do this once you're married. But you really can't set your mind on the things of heaven while your heart is fixated on the things of earth. As you wait on the Lord, don't lose your eternal focus. A proper focus will make the wait a lot easier.

WORKING FOR THE LORD

Now we're going to take this matter of being a Christian single person a little deeper, because God's viewpoint on singleness and marriage is different from the world's view, which we would expect. Unfortunately, God's view on singleness is also frequently different from the view singles are getting in the church, which should not be the case.

The world—and too often the church—treats singleness as an awkward, in-between stage from adolescence to marriage, a temporary stopover that tends to make singles feel like second-class citizens. But God views both singleness and marriage as *divine callings* in which we are to work for Him with all the commitment we can give.

To help you see this, I want to back up a bit in 1 Corinthians 7 and look at verses 20 and 24. Verse 20: "Each man must remain in that condition in which he was called." Verse 24: "Each one is to remain with God in that condition in which he was called."

These are two very important verses when it comes to the way your marital status relates to your calling as a Christian. The key in each verse is the word *condition.* In verse 20, this is actually the same Greek term as the word translated "called."

In other words, God is saying, "Remain in the calling to which you were called." This is significant because it equates our status as singles or marrieds with our calling. Verse 24 has the same idea because the word *condition* is in italics. That means it is not in the Greek text but was supplied by the translators. We could just as easily supply the word *calling* in verse 24 and get the proper sense of the passage.

What I'm saying is that your calling as a single person is not just the current status you happen to be in. It is part of your divine calling.

The problem today is that many singles have differentiated their status from their calling. This creates trouble because it can lead them to focus their energies on trying to change their marital status while missing their calling as singles.

If you are single, your singleness is not just *where you happen to be* right now. It's *where God has you right now,* and there's a world of difference between those two outlooks.

Your singleness is part of your calling from the Lord, your reason for being or your divinely ordained purpose. This doesn't mean you have to be in full-time Christian ministry. Your calling may involve serving as a physician or an accountant or whatever else for the glory and the kingdom of God. Once you see being single as a calling from God, you can give yourself to following and serving Him without anxiety about your future.

Now I know what many singles may be thinking at this point. They're afraid to accept singleness as a "calling" because it sounds like they're locking themselves into being unmarried the rest of their lives. But that's not necessarily true. God can alter your single status any time He chooses. The good news is that Christians can fulfill their calling whether they're single or married.

So what should you know in order to live victoriously as a single person while you work for the Lord? Let me give you three principles from God's Word.

God Wants You to Be Free

As he urged believers in Corinth to stay in their calling, Paul told the singles that those who marry "will have trouble in this life, and I am trying to spare you" (1 Corinthians 7:28). Later he said, "I want you to be free from concern" (v. 32).

God wants singles to stop worrying and obsessing about when and whom they will marry. He wants them to enjoy the freedom their status gives them to serve Him without distractions.

This is so important that I want to make a statement that may rock you back for a minute: If you are a Christian single who is preoccupied with getting married to the point that you are frustrated day in and day out, week in and week out, year in and year out, then you are living outside the will of God.

I say that because if this is true of you, you are living with a focus that God never meant you to have. God says you ought to be free from the distractions that marriage brings. Singles who are concentrating more on marriage than on living for God are like folk who talk on a cell phone while they're driving. You risk an accident if you try to do both at the same time.

Let's get it straight. In the context of 1 Corinthians 7, singles are the free ones while married people are bound. Now don't get too shook up at that. I'm having a little fun with the text here, but Paul does speak of married people as being "bound" with no idea of "release" (v. 27). And freedom does mean liberty from bondage.

So single believers are to be free from concern. But what concern? Paul explained further. "One who is unmarried is concerned about the things of the Lord, how he may please the Lord; but one who is married is concerned about the things of the world, how he may please his wife, and his interests are divided" (1 Corinthians 7:32–34a).

The distinction Paul made is important. He was not saying that married people don't care about pleasing the Lord in terms of being the Christian He wants them to be. God expects all believers to please Him regardless of marital status.

Instead, the idea of "pleasing the Lord" here has to do with fulfilling our calling. In that sense, it's true that married people have more issues to be concerned about than singles do. A single person can, for example, answer a call to the mission field or accept a job in a different locale without having to check with anyone, so to speak.

A young woman in our church once told me she was going to the mission field for a period of service while she had the opportunity. "Pastor," she said, "I may not be able to do this later if I get married."

Obviously, married people have their mates to consider in such decisions. And sometimes the task of blending two people with different personalities and ideas can produce a tension that every married couple has felt. As we saw earlier, Paul passed up his right to get married for the sake of his calling.

Single Christian, don't sacrifice the freedom you

have by acting like a married person. What I mean is that there are singles today who are so hung up on being married that they basically put themselves in the same situation as married people. That is, their attention is already as divided as if they were married, so they aren't truly fulfilling their calling as singles. They're free, but living as if they're bound.

When two people come together as one in marriage, they give up their right to act independently. The fact that they now have another person to care for also means that married couples must increase their focus on everyday needs and concerns, which Paul called "the things of the world" (vv. 33–34).

That's not a put-down, but a recognition of the fact that marriage requires a lot of time, commitment, and resources. The difference is between an earthly perspective and an eternal perspective. Desiring to be married is a noble desire, but God wants to make sure that Christians go into marriage with their eyes open to its demands, and not to seek marriage at the cost of their commitment to Him and their calling from Him.

The person who has the right perspective sees singleness as an advantage, not a disadvantage. It's an advantage from a kingdom perspective, not because marriage is bad but because it is distracting and brings with it concerns that a single person does not have.

So being unmarried offers single people an unusual degree of freedom to pursue God's calling for their lives. But that means Christian singles have a decision to make—whether to fulfill their calling or spend their time worrying about when Mr. or Miss Right is going to show up.

The biblical heroine Ruth is a great example of a single person who made the right decision. Ruth was a widow living in her native Moab with two other widows: her sister-in-law Orpah and her mother-in-law, Naomi, who had moved to Moab from Bethlehem.

God wants single believers to be set apart for His service.

If you're familiar with the story from the book of Ruth, you know that Naomi decided to go back to Israel and tried to send Ruth and Orpah back to their families in Moab because their chances of finding husbands in Israel were slim.

Orpah listened to Naomi and went back to her pagan people, but Ruth had another agenda. She had become a believer in the God of Israel, and she was determined to follow Him. That meant following Naomi back to Bethlehem even if it meant that Ruth would never marry again.

Now we know that God had a husband in mind for Ruth, but she didn't know that. She just wanted to serve God and take care of Naomi, which we could say was Ruth's calling from God.

Ruth made a spiritual decision, a theological choice based on her love for God, whereas Orpah made a social decision. Orpah disappeared from the scene, while Ruth became famous in Israel. We'll look at her story in more detail below.

The interesting thing is that Naomi the Israelite, who knew the true God, was more interested in trying to get Ruth and Orpah married off than she was in trying to encourage them to become true followers of God.

But Ruth had enough sense to understand that her calling from God superceded her marital status. Ruth freely decided to go back to Bethlehem with Naomi, even though as far as she knew only poverty and singleness awaited her. At that point Ruth was truly free to follow God, and God was free to work miraculously in her life.

Too many Christian singles are listening to too many Naomis, who are trying to get them married off instead of encouraging them to fulfill their divine calling. God wants you to be free in your singleness, so don't let other people set your agenda or try to rush you into marriage.

God Wants You to Function

God not only wants you to be free as a single person, but He wants you to use that freedom to function for His kingdom. God wants single believers to be set apart for His service.

Being set apart is the basic meaning of the word

holy, as Paul wrote in 1 Corinthians 7:34: "The woman who is unmarried, and the virgin, is concerned about the things of the Lord, that she may be holy both in body and spirit."

Now again, don't misunderstand. Every believer is to be set apart for God's service, and married Christians are also called to be holy in body and spirit. But Paul was emphasizing the unique opportunity that unmarried people have to focus their time and energies on serving the Lord.

So single Christians need to answer the question of how well they are using their unique freedom to function in a way that contributes to God's kingdom. Is there a direct correlation between what you do every day and the calling you have to fulfill God's purpose for you? Or are you allowing the world to distract you from your divine calling and function?

Whenever I teach on this, I think of the story that was told about Yogi Berra, the great catcher for the New York Yankees, and Hank Aaron, baseball's all-time home-run king.

The story goes that as Aaron came to bat in the All-Star Game one time, Berra was doing all he could to distract the great slugger. Berra was a chatterbox behind the plate who was always trying to distract the hitters, so he said to Aaron, "Hey Hank, you're holding your bat the wrong way. You should have the label turned up so you can read it." But Aaron ignored Berra and said nothing.

Yogi wouldn't give up, however. "Hank, I'm telling

you, you're holding the bat the wrong way. The label should be turned where you can read it." But still Aaron said nothing.

After this had gone on for several pitches, Aaron suddenly hit the next pitch out of the park for a home run. As he crossed home plate, he said to Berra, "Yogi, I came up here to hit, not to read."

You and I need to know why we are here. We need to say, "I came here to hit home runs." Don't let other people distract you from your calling, or you'll be standing at home plate messing with the bat instead of swinging for the fences.

What was Adam doing when he found a wife? He wasn't out girl-watching, because there were no other human beings around. He wasn't daydreaming about his wedding day. Adam was busy functioning in his God-given role of tending the Garden of Eden and, more specifically, naming the animals when God put him to sleep and removed a rib to fashion Eve (see Genesis 2:19–22).

Now I want you to notice that as Adam functioned in his calling, God used that situation to create the scenario in which He introduced Adam to his mate. As Adam named each animal he noticed that, for example, for every Mr. Gorilla there was a Mrs. Gorilla. In other words, every animal had its mate. But there was no one who corresponded to Adam.

So by the time Adam had finished naming the animals, it was abundantly clear that there was no one for him. The Bible even says, "But for Adam there was not found a helper suitable for him" (Genesis 2:20). By the time Adam had finished his work and noticed his need, God was ready to supply him with a mate.

God does not want you sitting around fretting about your wedding day. He wants you functioning for Him until He creates your wedding day.

Too many singles are like people going for a Sunday drive. Our parents used to take us for Sunday drives in the afternoon. The goal was just to go, not to go anywhere in particular. That was fun for a while, but then it became boring.

Are you going through life aimlessly, or do you have a mission and sense of calling on your life? Do you have a passion from God that motivates you? If you are a single Christian it's because God has you single, and you ought to know why He wants you to function in this calling for whatever period He deems right.

It's easy to get bogged down in endless activity that doesn't take you anywhere. Single people have a unique freedom to find and pursue God's purpose for them and to function in that calling with undivided, undistracted commitment to Christ.

God Wants to Change Your Focus

Living freely and fully for Christ as an unmarried believer will require a change of your focus from preoccupation with marriage to preoccupation with Christ.

Paul wrote in 1 Corinthians 7:35, "This I say for your own benefit; not to put a restraint upon you, but to promote what is appropriate and to secure undistracted devotion to the Lord." The only way to avoid distractions is to keep your focus in the right place.

Paul was not trying to put handcuffs on single Christians and keep the two sexes apart. He wasn't trying to prevent people from desiring to get married or pursuing matrimony. He was not antimarriage at all. But there was a benefit in being single that Paul wanted to make sure his readers understood.

We've been talking about this benefit, which is stated here as "undistracted devotion to the Lord." One way Satan robs us of God's best is to cause a disturbance in our lives to distract us, much the way one thief may distract a store clerk so the other thief can steal goods or money without being noticed.

The devil has so many Christian singles so disturbed and worried about their marital status that he's running amok through their lives, stealing their joy and robbing them of their effectiveness for Christ. When your focus shifts from Christ to yourself, that means a thief is at work on you.

This reminds me of an incident that happened several years ago in the Goodwill Games, which were being held in Edmonton, Canada. During the four-by-one-hundred relay, a Jamaican athlete who was to run the third leg of the race for his team allowed his attention to wander as he waited for the baton to be passed.

This man happened to look up at the big screen that was televising another event and saw a friend of his getting ready to compete. The runner stared at the screen for just a few seconds, but as he did so his teammate came running up to him with the baton. Instead of a smooth handoff, the incoming runner collided with his distracted teammate, and the race was over for the Jamaican team.

The message for us is clear. We need to stop looking at other people's races and start running our own race. For singles, this includes keeping your focus on God instead of always looking around trying to find a partner. God is saying to single believers, "Focus on Me, and I will do your looking for you."

If you live in a large metropolitan area like Dallas where the roads always seem to be under construction and clogged with traffic, you learn that it doesn't pay to go very far without tuning in to the latest traffic report.

Many traffic reports include a helicopter that allows the reporter to see beyond the traffic tie-ups on the ground and give drivers the big picture, including warnings of trouble ahead and alternate routes. When you are tuned in to the person in the helicopter, you hear things that other people who are in too much of a hurry to listen don't get to hear.

That's what focusing on the Lord does for believers. When you are tuned in to the Lord in terms of undivided devotion to Him, you'll hear things that other people won't hear because the antenna of your heart is up and listening.

I love the story of the businessman and the Native American who were walking down a noisy street in the city one day. Suddenly, the Native American stopped and said, "Shhh. Listen!"

The businessman said, "Listen for what?"

"Don't you hear it?" the Native American asked. "It's a cricket."

The businessman said, "A cricket? I don't hear anything."

But the Native American looked around and saw a cricket on the sidewalk. He reached down, picked it up, and showed it to the businessman, who was amazed. "I don't believe it. Here we are downtown with all this noise and all these people, and you hear a cricket. How did you do that?"

"I'll show you," the other man said. He took some change out of his pocket and threw it on the sidewalk. As the money clattered and rolled around, twenty people stopped to look. "You always hear what you're tuned to hear," the Native American said.

A lot of singles will never find their mate because they're tuned to their friends or the dating scene or something else instead of being tuned in to God. But He's the only One who knows how to get Adam and Eve hooked up.

Single Christian, if you will set your focus on God and function for Him in the freedom He has given you, you won't have to worry about Him finding you when He's ready to hook you up with someone. Look to God, and let Him do your looking for you.

One day I was at the airport trying to get to my gate for the flight out when I heard my name announced over the intercom: "Dr. Tony Evans, please go to the nearest white courtesy phone for a message."

Now I was concentrating on something else because I had a flight to make and a destination to reach, so it took a few seconds for the reality to sink in that I was the one being paged. I went to the nearest phone and received a message from my administrative assistant, who needed to contact me and knew I was still at the airport because she makes my travel arrangements.

My point is that this phone call found me in the middle of thousands of people who also had flights to make and plans to keep. I was doing what I was called to do, on my way to minister the Word of God to people. I didn't go to the airport to hang out and wait for a call from my assistant.

But when she needed to reach me, it was no problem because she knew where I was and because the airport has a system in place to reach travelers with important messages. And the fact that I was immersed in a sea of people in the middle of a noisy terminal was no obstacle at all.

God has sent you to the airport because He wants to take you somewhere and has a plan in mind to get you there. And when you as a single Christian decide that you are going to focus on Christ and His plan for you, if God wants to interrupt your plans and call your name with a message, He knows how to reach you.

In the meantime, your job is to keep your focus on the Lord and keep moving ahead with His plan for you. It's when you're going somewhere with the Lord, getting ready to fly high with Him, that He is freed up to make a connection with you and for you.

WEDDED IN THE LORD

I want to conclude our study on singleness by considering some important principles that single believers need to know as they consider a possible marriage in their future.

It's safe to assume that the majority of single people, at least those still in the "twenty-something" category, hope and expect to be married someday. And despite all the twisted views of morality in our day, marriage is still the norm for most people.

That's good, because God created marriage and holds it in high esteem. But as I have pointed out, the Bible also makes it clear that those who are not married have not somehow fallen into a second-class-citizen status in the kingdom.

In 1 Corinthians 7, Paul's great chapter on singleness and marriage, he concluded by dealing with the case of a single person who desires to get married (vv. 36–40). This person may have never been married, or may be single again after a divorce or the death of a spouse.

God's Word has a word for each of these cases—and along the way Paul even adds a special word to people who are now married. I call these three categories those who are single, those who wish they were single, and those who are single again.

A Word to the Single

The first category of singleness Paul addressed is those who have never been married. "If any man thinks that he is acting unbecomingly toward his virgin daughter, if she is past her youth, and if it must be so, let him do what he wishes, he does not sin; let her marry" (1 Corinthians 7:36).

This is a message to fathers whose single daughters are feeling their biological clock ticking and want to get married. A father in this case is not to try to prevent his daughter's marriage. Now this assumes that the father has had input into the choice of a potential marriage partner, a major point we'll deal with in a minute.

Before we move to that, I want you to see verses 37–38, which answer the question of what happens when a single woman is content to remain so and the father thinks this is the best option: "But he who stands firm in his heart, being under no constraint, but has authority over his own will, and has decided this in his own heart, to keep his own virgin daughter, he will do well. So then both he who gives his own virgin daughter in marriage does well, and he who does not give her in marriage will do better."

This case presupposes that the daughter is also content to remain single, since it's hard to imagine a caring father refusing to honor his daughter's legitimate desires to get married and deciding to keep her single against her wishes. A woman who is not worried about getting married shouldn't be pressured by others because singleness is a perfectly acceptable choice—and even "better" in the context of being free to serve Christ.

But we're assuming the case of a single person who

desires to get married. When Paul talked about a father who "gives" his daughter in marriage, he had a lot more in mind than we normally think of.

In today's culture, a father sometimes doesn't even meet his daughter's future husband until the two are already serious, and then dad's job is limited to paying the wedding bills and walking his daughter down the aisle to answer the preacher's question, "Who gives this woman to be married to this man?"

Things were radically different in biblical days. Paul was writing in a context in which marriages were typically arranged by the parents. In the biblical world, there was no thought that parents would not be involved in the marriage of their children.

That's because the family was viewed as a continuum from one generation to another, not as a bunch of isolated units who happened to be related. The continuation and well-being of the family was in part dependent on how successful each generation was in establishing solid marriages and homes.

And so if a daughter in this context wanted to get married, her father was to get involved in the process of selecting and approving a potential mate. There's a lot here to deal with, and you may already be raising questions, so stay with me. I think the following discussion will deal with the pertinent issues.

First of all, as we saw earlier, the Bible tells singles not to be out wife- or husband-hunting (see 1 Corinthians 7:27). This doesn't mean a single person can't meet others and establish relationships. The idea is not to buy into the world's mentality that there's something wrong if you're not married, or depend on the world's methods of finding a mate.

So if a woman wants to get married, whom should she tell first of all? Her father, because he is to be actively involved in the process.

Why? For a number of reasons. A young woman's father is, or should be, the one man in her life who has her deepest interests at heart, who has been given the responsibility of being her spiritual leader, and who is in the position to evaluate a possible husband's fitness from a man's perspective and discern the direction and potential of his life.

Now you may be saying, "Come on, Tony, you're not saying we should go back to arranged marriages, are you? This is the twenty-first century, not the first century."

Well, my answer to that question depends on what is meant by arranged marriages. If we're talking about cases in which two fathers, or two sets of parents, get together and pledge their children to each other before the two have met or even grown up, that's not going to happen in our culture (although it still happens in other countries—with success, we should note). But if we are talking about serious parental involvement and approval in the mate-selection process, then yes, this is the norm that the Bible teaches.

Some would say that this was no more than a social custom, the way they did it in Paul's day. But this is not the case. The principle of a father giving his daughter in marriage, in the biblical sense of preparing her for that marriage, was laid down at the first marriage when God created Eve and "brought her" to Adam (Genesis 2:22).

God the Father walked Eve down the aisle, so to speak, and presented her to Adam, establishing the pattern that we still use in marriage ceremonies today. I'd like to suggest this is a theological matter and not merely a social custom. The Father approved his daughter's marriage, and then validated it by giving her away.

In fact, I believe that every unmarried woman ought to have a male looking out for her marital interests. Ideally, that should be her father. But many fathers are absent today, and some others who are present are either not believers or are not spiritually attuned.

In cases where believing women do not have a father who can fill that role, the church is to act as a father and look after their spiritual and marital interests. The Bible speaks of the church leaders as fathers among the body of Christ (see 1 Corinthians 4:14–15; 1 Thessalonians 2:11).

What happens when the single person in question is a son and not a daughter? Many of the same principles apply, because sons also need to benefit from the wisdom and instruction of their parents. The New Testament doesn't address this issue directly as it does for women, but clearly a young man who has a godly father and mother would do well to heed their advice and follow their spiritual leadership.

Of course, arranged marriages in biblical days did

involve sons. The classic example is Abraham sending his servant to find a bride for Isaac (Genesis 24:1–4), in this case a young woman named Rebekah whom Isaac didn't even meet until the marriage had been arranged.

Since we're dealing with single women in the text before us in 1 Corinthians 7, let's talk about a father's role in helping his daughter to marry in the Lord. One reason for a father's involvement is to make sure that his daughter doesn't marry a man who turns out to be a fool.

A younger person may be swayed by the externals, by the front that the other person puts up. But a godly father who is walking with the Lord can help his daughter see the real deal in a potential husband, and he can demand some serious commitments from the man who desires to marry his daughter.

When I married my wife, Lois, her father had me write a letter outlining my basic commitments, and he still has it on file. My two sons-in-law had to write similar letters, which are in my file. We had to have some meetings and come to some basic agreements before they married my daughters.

Single Christian woman, if you have a father who walks with the Lord and you are thinking about marrying someone your father doesn't agree with, you are taking a massive risk. If you and your dad are on the same page spiritually and are committed to the Lord, then He is going to validate your marital choice through your father.

With women's full entry into the workforce, and more people waiting longer to get married, many single women today are successfully established on their own. Sometimes a woman in this position will meet a man who doesn't have a regular job, drives an old beat-up car, and is still living with his mama.

Now what this woman doesn't need is someone who will take her backward, or a guy who is only looking for someone to pay all of his bills. So there needs to be some evaluation of his situation, and a father can help his daughter measure this man's potential and his spiritual condition.

For example, maybe this man isn't where he wants to be right now, but he's showing signs of moving in the right direction. He may be in school working toward a degree, or he's having to overcome some hard circumstances. A woman needs her father to help her evaluate a potential husband objectively because if she is in love with the guy, she may not see all of these things or may overlook some caution signs.

A father is in a good position to evaluate marriage potential because he knows what is involved in fulfilling the biblical instruction for a man to leave his father and mother and cleave to his wife.

The Bible only speaks of a woman leaving her parents by implication in respect to the man leaving his parents. The reason is that a woman is always to be covered and protected by authority. She is to be covered by her biological father, or a spiritual substitute, until such time as she is given away in marriage to a man who is pledged to cover and protect her. A woman who desires to be married needs to take seriously the Bible's admonition to follow God's order and line of authority through her father.

A Word to Those Who Wish They Were Single

We also need to address another group of people—those who aren't single, but wish they were. These are people who say they didn't realize what they were getting into when they got married, and now they want out. The unfortunate fact is that plenty of married people wish they were single again.

These may be cases in which it is better to be single than to be married. It's better to be single wanting to be married than it is to be married wanting to be single. You can change your single status, but you aren't to undo a marriage simply because you want out.

Once you're married you are bound to your mate for life.

Paul stated an important principle of marriage when he wrote, "A wife is bound as long as her husband lives" (1 Corinthians 7:39a). We've talked about the bondage of marriage versus the freedom of singleness, so we won't go there again.

Folks need to understand what they are agreeing to when they say, "I do," because too many married people *don't* anymore. But partners in a marriage are bound to each other as long as they both live, because the principle works both ways. Marriage is easy to get into, but hard to get out of because you are bound.

Now I know we have no-fault divorce today, although some legislatures are trying to change things and make it harder to get divorced. Society may recognize divorce for incompatibility or irreconcilable differences, but God doesn't recognize either of these reasons. So although the judge downtown may declare you divorced in such cases, in God's eyes you are still married.

A single person may say, "Hey, you're scaring me about getting married." Good! If you're single, you'd better be sober-minded and a little scared about making this commitment, because once you're married you are bound to your mate for life.

Jesus once delivered some straight teaching on marriage and divorce in which He said that contrary to the popular view, it wasn't OK for a man to divorce his wife for any reason.

When Jesus was finished, His disciples said, "If the relationship of the man with his wife is like this, it is better not to marry" (Matthew 19:10). In other words, Jesus had scared them about being married, and He didn't back off. We need to do some serious and sober thinking about singleness and marriage.

A Word to Those Who Are Single Again

Let's read on in 1 Corinthians 7:39. The Bible says, "But if her husband is dead, she is free to be married to whom she wishes, only in the Lord." To close our study on singleness, we need to discuss the case of those who were once married and are now single again.

The Bible only grants freedom from a marriage when the death of a spouse occurs. Now let me add that the Bible recognizes two kinds of death that can end a marriage. The first and most obvious is physical death, which clearly sets the living partner free from the marriage. There is no disagreement here, so we can move on to the issue of spiritual death.

When God warned Adam not to eat from the forbidden tree, He said, "In the day that you eat from it you will surely die" (Genesis 2:17). Now the day Adam and Eve ate of the fruit, they did not drop dead physically, but they did die spiritually, and their relationship with God was broken.

The Bible recognizes the reality of spiritual death and the separation that it brings in a relationship. Jesus said divorce was wrong "except for immorality" (Matthew 19:9), which brings death to a marriage. The Bible says that when there is sexual immorality, which is a form of spiritual death, the marriage dies. There can be forgiveness and restoration, but immorality clearly introduces spiritual death into a marriage.

But the Word does not limit spiritual death to immorality within a marriage. On a broader scale it can include any lifestyle by any Christian that is contrary to the truth and detrimental to the kingdom of God. One example is found in 1 Corinthians 5:11, where Paul mentioned such things as drunkenness and swindling people.

So how can it be determined if a marriage is dead and a divorce can be granted without violating God's Word? The death must be recognized by the church, which pronounces that the union is dead and issues the death certificate. In the case of the incestuous man in 1 Corinthians 6, the church should have judged him because the church is God's court and God's coroner to determine if a death has occurred.

The point of 1 Corinthians 6 is that the church is to act on God's behalf in matters that we normally take to the judge downtown. The church court should be a believer's first court of appeal in a dispute. If a married person believes that his or her marriage is spiritually dead, that person should appeal to the church for a judgment. Our church in Dallas holds a church court every week to deal with matters that come up.

In the case of marriage and divorce, the problem is that many people don't want to go to the church court because it's too tough. They want to go downtown, where it's easy to get a divorce. But God doesn't recognize a divorce until the church recognizes that spiritual death exists in the marriage, that one partner has been unfaithful or has developed a totally rebellious, unrepentant attitude.

I realize this is more involved than we can discuss

fully in this brief context. But I want you to see that it takes death to dissolve a marriage and set a married person free to marry again.

You may be wondering why this is such a big deal. Let me encourage you to read Malachi 2:14–16, in which God told the people of Israel that He hated divorce and that because they were divorcing their mates illegitimately He would not hear their prayers. Anyone who divorces for the wrong reasons leaves God standing at the altar too, because He says He won't listen to them.

But when a death has occurred in the marriage, the remaining spouse is free to remarry "in the Lord." There is freedom of choice within that boundary.

What does it mean to be married in the Lord? Two concepts are at work here. The first is the stipulation that the person being considered for marriage needs to be a Christian. A believer and an unbeliever are never to be joined together in any close coequal partnership, including marriage.

The Bible says this in 2 Corinthians 6:14–15, where Paul warned, "Do not be bound together with unbelievers; for what partnership have righteousness and lawlessness, or what fellowship has light with darkness? Or what harmony has Christ with Belial, or what has a believer in common with an unbeliever?"

This concept actually comes from Deuteronomy 22:10, where God told Israel not to put an ox and a donkey together in the same yoke because they are different animals that won't be pulling together. They were not created to work together.

This is the picture of a Christian and a non-Christian joining together in marriage. They will not be pulling together equally, and they are going to have problems.

A single man was at the airport one day when he met a nice woman. They began talking and really began to click with each other. Something was happening; a fire was starting to ignite.

Finally the man asked the woman where she was flying to. It turned out she was flying north to Canada, while he was flying south to Mexico. He wanted the two of them to fly together, but it was impossible because they were going in opposite directions.

If you're a Christian you are heading in the opposite direction from an unbeliever, and the two of you can't be yoked together without someone getting hurt. This is one area where far too many Christian singles are willing to compromise in order to get married. But the Bible forbids marriage between a believer and a lost person under any circumstance. Someone has said that if you marry a child of the devil, you're going to have in-law problems.

The idea of marrying in the Lord and being equally joined with another Christian also has a deeper facet to it. You should not only marry a Christian, but a Christian who is pulling in the same direction as you.

It's one thing to get married to a Christian, but it's another thing to marry a Christian whose spiritual desires and commitments complement yours instead of contradicting them.

For example, if you are committed to grow in your

faith and you're moving in that direction, you are going to want someone who wants to grow in Christ too.

Earlier we used the example of a single person who feels called to the mission field. If you have such a desire, and you meet another Christian who has no inkling at all that God is calling him or her to the mission field, this difference ought to cause the two of you to go very slowly in your relationship. Otherwise, you may wind up pulling in different directions.

As a single Christian, you have three choices.

This doesn't mean that two people who want to get married must be alike in everything. That will never happen in the first place, and if it did they would be in for a very boring relationship. But it's important that their differences are at least in the same direction.

So the desire for marriage is legitimate. But Paul concluded his extended teaching on this subject by saying, "In my opinion she [a widow] is happier if she remains as she is; and I think that I also have the Spirit of God" (1 Corinthians 7:40). This was not just a human opinion, but the revealed Word and will of God. In other words, Paul wasn't just telling his personal bias, but was speaking under the Spirit's inspiration.

Single Christian—widow, widower, never married, or divorced—my word of counsel to you is don't be in a hurry to get married. Don't rush the process or rush off to the altar with someone who may not be God's choice simply because you're afraid you may not get another chance. Don't be in such a hurry that you crash and burn.

Let me remind you again of Ruth, who was a widow and successful. Ruth determined to pursue God, even if it meant giving up the legitimate pursuit of a husband and the security of marriage.

Ruth went back to Israel with Naomi, assuming she would never get married again because she was a foreigner from Moab. But as she fulfilled her calling and served the Lord, the day came when she happened to glean in the fields of Boaz—and one of the Bible's great love stories began to unfold.

Ruth was in an obscure position, and humanly speaking was about as far from having marriage prospects as any woman in her day. But when God was ready, He found her, or rather, He made sure that Boaz found her.

But let me point out that the story of Ruth is not the story of a single woman getting married. It is the story of two people who were used of God to carry on the line of the Messiah. Obed, the son born to Ruth and Boaz, was the father of Jesse, who was the father of David, through whom came Jesus Christ!

God may have you single right now, but He may be preparing you for something that is much bigger than you could imagine!

Let me give you a helpful formula for approaching single life. As a single Christian, you have three choices. Your first choice is to *gripe* about your lot and the lack of suitable potential mates and gripe that you aren't married because you can feel your biological clock ticking.

A second choice is to *grab* the next available person who comes along, regardless of that person's fitness for marriage. That's a bad choice, as we have seen.

A third choice for you as a Christian single is to *grow* in grace and in your walk with the Lord. You can say to God, "I am going to walk with You no matter what, and I am going to trust You and wait on You for Your timing in my life."

What will your choice be? May the Lord give you grace to follow Him.

THE URBAN ALTERNATIVE

The Philosophy

Dr. Tony Evans and TUA believe the answer to transforming our culture comes from the inside out and from the bottom up. We believe the core cause of the problems we face is a spiritual one; therefore, the only way to address them is spiritually. And that means the proclamation and application of biblical principles to the four areas of life—the individual, the family, the church, and the community. We've tried a political, social, economic, and even a religious agenda. It's time for a kingdom agenda.

The Purpose

We believe that when each biblical sphere of life functions properly, the net result is evangelism, discipleship, and community impact. As people learn how to govern themselves under God, they then transform the institutions of family, church, and government from a biblically based kingdom perspective.

The Programs

To achieve our goal we use a variety of strategies, methods, and resources for reaching and equipping as many people as possible.

- Broadcast Media
  The Urban Alternative reaches hundreds of thousands of people each day with a kingdom-based approach to life through its daily radio program, weekly television broadcast, and the Internet.

- Leadership Training
  Our national Church Development Conference, held annually, equips pastors and lay leaders to become agents of change. Teaching biblical methods of church ministry has helped congregations renew their sense of mission and expand their ministry impact.

- Crusades/Conferences
  Crusades are designed to bring churches together across racial, cultural, and denominational lines to win the lost. TUA also seeks to keep these churches together for ongoing fellowship and community impact. Conferences give Christians practical biblical insight on how to live victoriously in accordance with God's Word and His kingdom agenda in the four areas of life—personal, family, church, and community.

- Resource Development
  We are fostering lifelong learning partnerships with the people we serve by providing a variety of published materials. We offer books, audiotapes,

videos, and booklets to strengthen people in their walk with God and ministry to others.

- Project Turn-Around
PTA is a comprehensive church-based community impact strategy. It addresses such areas as economic development, education, housing, health revitalization, family renewal and reconciliation. To model the success of the project, TUA invests in its own program locally. We also assist other churches in tailoring the model to meet the specific needs of their communities, while simultaneously addressing the spiritual and moral frame of reference.

* * *

For more information, a catalog of Dr. Tony Evans's ministry resources, and a complimentary copy of Dr. Evans's monthly devotional magazine,
call (800) 800-3222 or
write TUA at P.O. Box 4000, Dallas TX 75208.
or log on to TonyEvans.org.

MARRIAGE MATTERS

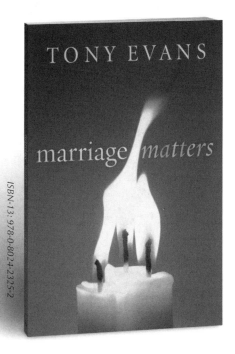

ISBN-13: 978-0-8024-2325-2

Marriage Matters examines the nature of the covenant, or agreement, we enter into on our wedding day. This booklet provides the foundation for the booklets For Married Women Only and For Married Men Only, as Evans looks to the Scriptures to define what a covenant is, who makes it, and what the implications are. Let the practical and engaging Tony Evans lead you in knowing just how much . . . Marriage Matters.

MOODY
PUBLISHERS
moodypublishers.com

FOR MARRIED MEN ONLY

FOR MARRIED WOMEN ONLY

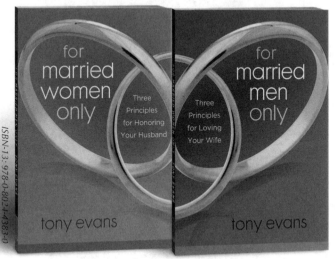

ISBN-13: 978-0-8024-4383-0

ISBN-13: 978-0-8024-4382-3

How is a wife to love her husband? By learning three things, says Tony Evans: how to submit, seduce, and surrender to her husband. Out of these three principles a godly marriage will grow. Straight-forward yet encouraging.

What does it mean for a husband to love his wife? Three things, says Tony Evans: a husband must be his wife's savior, sanctifier, and satisfier. It is by living out these three principles that a godly marriage will blossom and flourish.

MOODY
PUBLISHERS
moodypublishers.com

Other books in the *Tony Evans Speaks Out Series*

Sexual Purity	978-0-8024-4387-8
Single Parenting	978-0-8024-4388-5
Divorce & Remarriage	978-0-8024-4386-1
Gambling & the Lottery	978-0-8024-4385-4
Spiritual Warfare	978-0-8024-4369-4
Fasting	978-0-8024-4366-3
Heaven & Hell	978-0-8024-4367-0
Prayer	978-0-8024-4368-7